The Blue Egg

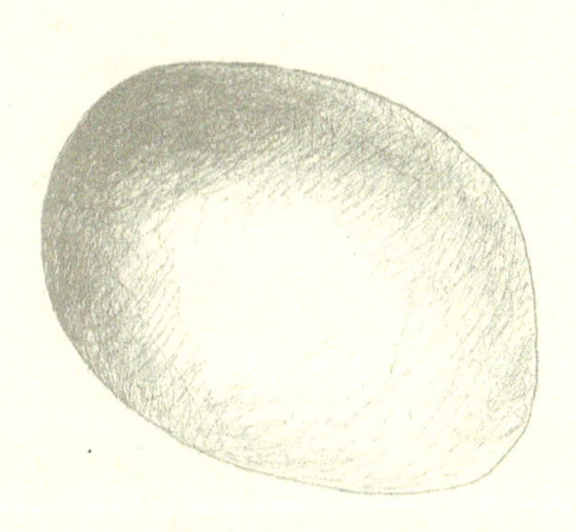

The Blue Egg

A Memoir
by
Nancy Hopkins Reily

Illustrated by Byron Jones

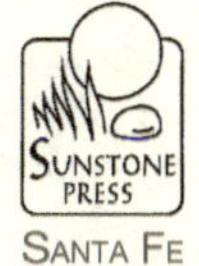

Santa Fe

Sunstone books may be purchased for educational, business, or sales promotional use.
For information please write: Special Markets Department, Sunstone Press,
P.O. Box 2321, Santa Fe, New Mexico 87504-2321.

Book and cover design › Vicki Ahl
Body typeface › Goudy OldStyle   Display type › Mona Lisa
Printed on acid-free paper
♾
eBook 978-1-61139-528-0

Library of Congress Cataloging-in-Publication Data

Names: Reily, Nancy Hopkins, 1934- author.
Title: The blue egg : a memoir / by Nancy Hopkins Reily ; illustrated by Byron Jones.
Description: Santa Fe : Sunstone Press, 2017.
Identifiers: LCCN 2017037233 (print) | LCCN 2017041864 (ebook) | ISBN 9781611395280 | ISBN 9781632932020 (softcover : alk. paper)
Subjects: LCSH: Reily, Nancy Hopkins, 1934- | Authors, American--20th century--Biography. | O'Keeffe, Georgia, 1887-1986. | O'Keeffe, Georgia, 1887-1986--Themes, motives.
Classification: LCC PS3568.E4853 (ebook) | LCC PS3568.E4853 Z46 2017 (print) | DDC 818/.603 [B] --dc23
LC record available at https://lccn.loc.gov/2017037233

WWW.SUNSTONEPRESS.COM
SUNSTONE PRESS / POST OFFICE BOX 2321 / SANTA FE, NM 87504-2321 /USA
(505) 988-4418 / ORDERS ONLY (800) 243-5644 / FAX (505) 988-1025

Dedicated
to my beautiful daughter,
Donna Carolyn Reily Davis

Thanks to my daughter, Donna Reily Davis, for suggesting I write of this journey, to Martha R. Chandler who read and commented on the first version, and to Byron Jones who provided his artistic, illustrative talent.

Thanks to James Clois Smith, Jr. who welcomed me with his expertise, to Carl Condit who answered all my questions, and to Vicki Ahl who with her design brought the text to life.

Contents

List of Illustrations

An egg is an egg.

An egg is an egg until it becomes a blue egg representing something else.

An egg is an egg until I see its ovoid shape as self expression.

The egg that becomes blue, ovoid, and self expression teaches me.

What is the Blue Egg?

Preface

The cold, crisp air added sparkle to the nine small bonfires in the Abiquiu, New Mexico plaza as we walked into Georgia O'Keeffe's house on Christmas Eve in 1953. My two brothers, Robert and Morten, and I were spending Christmas with our Aunt Helen and Uncle Winfield Morten at their Rancho de Abiquiu across the Chama River from Abiquiu. My mother and father were unable to be in our Dallas home for Christmas because my father was living with his cancer treatment in Iowa City, Iowa. My mother remained at his side and my aunt and uncle provided substitute parents.

As a guest in Georgia's home I sat quietly and properly on a *banco* and the white walls seemed seamless and simple except for a painting hanging on one wall. It, too, was white with a big blue ovoid shape in the middle. I struggled to see what it was and decided it must have been an unfinished painting or a painting of a blue egg.

As we left that evening the Blue Egg painting lingered in my memory for many years. The journey to discover the Blue Egg began unbeknownst to me that night amidst Georgia and my family.

I often wondered why I was so persistently intent on finding the Blue Egg. Why did it take root in my mind and remain? The true meaning was finally revealed in a timely manner.

1

Georgia's Home on the Prairie

Once upon a cold November Wisconsin day in 1887, Georgia Totto O'Keeffe was born. One of seven children, she lived in a farm house three and one-half miles southeast of Sun Prairie where the flat marshland prairie and rolling expanses met the blaze of the blue sky.

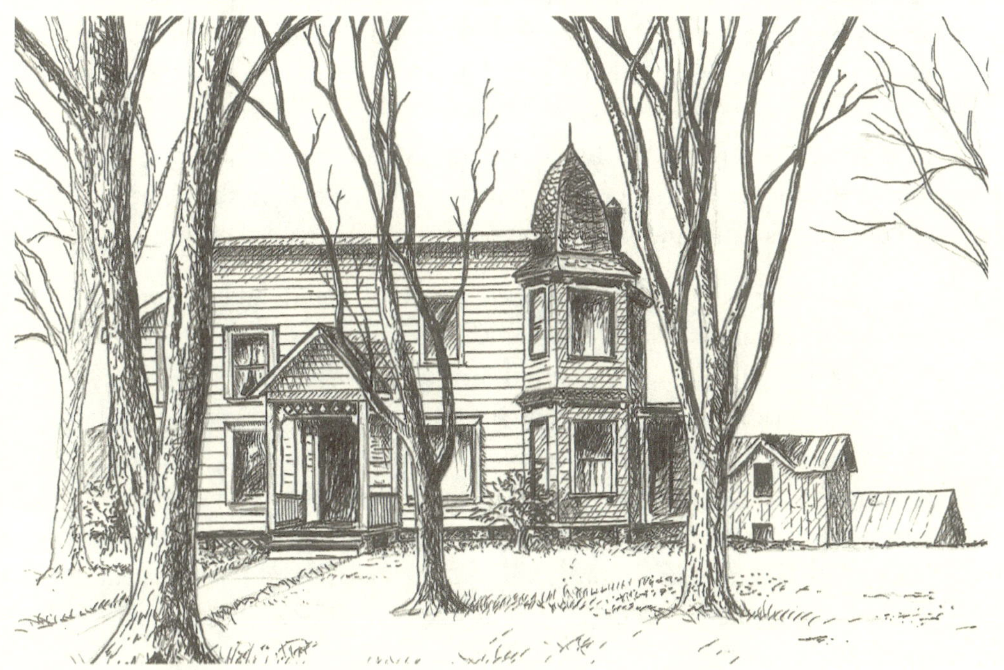

Georgia's Home on the Prairie

After the cold of November, in the spring Georgia, at eight or nine months of age propped up by big white pillows, sat on a handmade cotton patchwork quilt of two different materials: white background with very small red stars sprinkled over it quite close together, and black background with a red and white flower on it. To her it was the intensity, varieties of colors, and brightness of light. This was the beginning of many visual perceptions of seeing into the heart of her surroundings. Years later, to her mother Ida's amazement, Georgia recalled the exact color and design of the quilt. It was like Georgia's memory for the design was stitched tight like the thread on the quilt.

Ida, as a strong, individual mother, read aloud to Georgia and her six siblings the stories by James Fenimore Cooper (1789–1851) known as the first true American novelist. His boyhood spent in the wilds of the forests and mountains aroused his curiosity. In his writings he described the American forests, Great Lakes, and High Plains. Georgia heard the words and in her imagination they imparted a musical rhythm like a bird's wing fluttering. Georgia in her mind pictured the everyday words as reality because the nearby Sun Prairie lands encouraged her imagination. From the cultural patterns she experienced at home, Georgia sensed her art was the word's final destination. Georgia longed to cross the forest, walk in the desert, and see the heights. The land had no footprint until she stepped on it.

In doing so, Georgia developed a love of nature and fondness for the land where she saw and absorbed their colors and shapes. The primary colors of red, yellow, and blue would turn to secondary colors of green, orange, and violet mixed with the neutrals of white, black, and gray. The colors became warm and cool in her mind. The shapes were easily identified as straight lines, circles, ovals, domes, triangles, zigzags, and even pyramids. She relegated shapes to two dimensions rather than three dimensions because two dimensions appeared more manageable, compact, and less threatening. The message in her mind of colors and shapes would blend into a sense of wholeness.

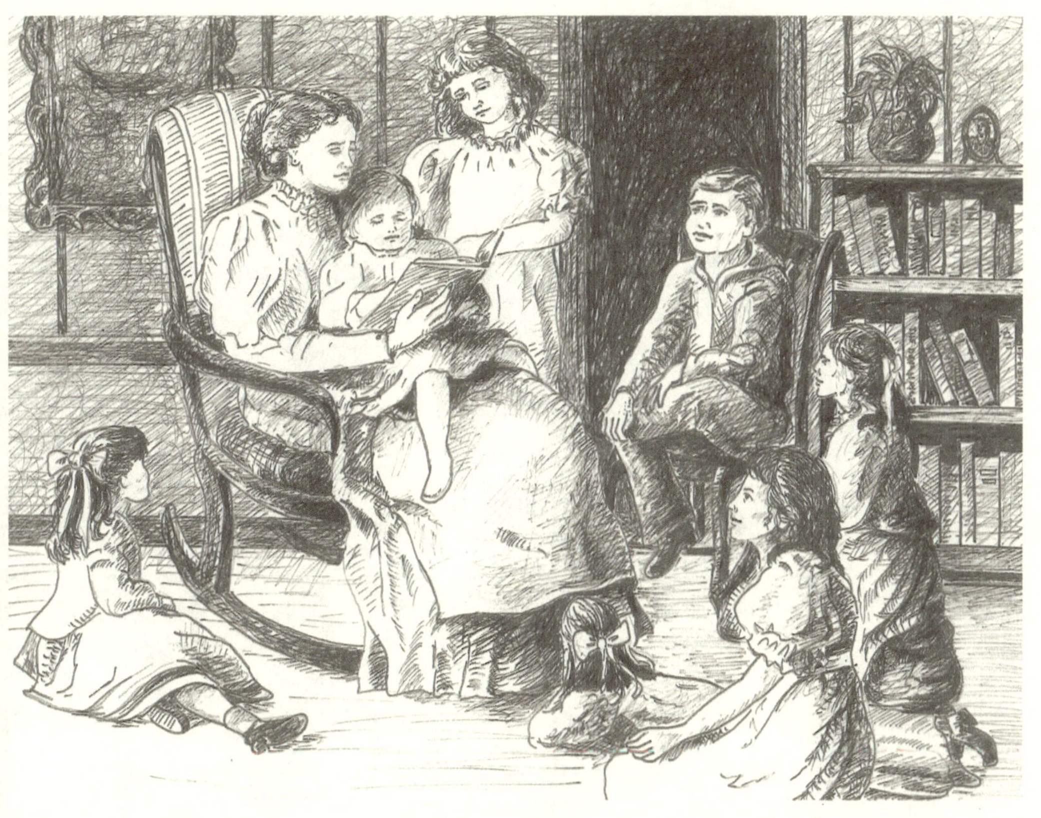

Georgia's Mother Reading James Fenimore Cooper to Her Children

Georgia understood the prairie's vast form, the sound of rain, the formation and shape of the clouds, the wind that she could not see and that left no shadow, the raindrops that were jewels from the sky, the unannounced first frost, the noise from the trees swaying, and the colors of the seasons when spring snow stumbles into summer sun. Her interest was uninterrupted, never wavering, as she walked on the land, and saw the variance of the land.

The birth of Georgia's creativity came like the birth of a child–when it was time. When Georgia was twelve years old in 1899, she envisioned herself being an artist. Even then she could have easily held in her hand an artist's palette displaying colors in a variety of shapes. That year Georgia had a defining moment as if she already had such a palette of colors in her hand and said to a childhood friend, "I want to be an artist."

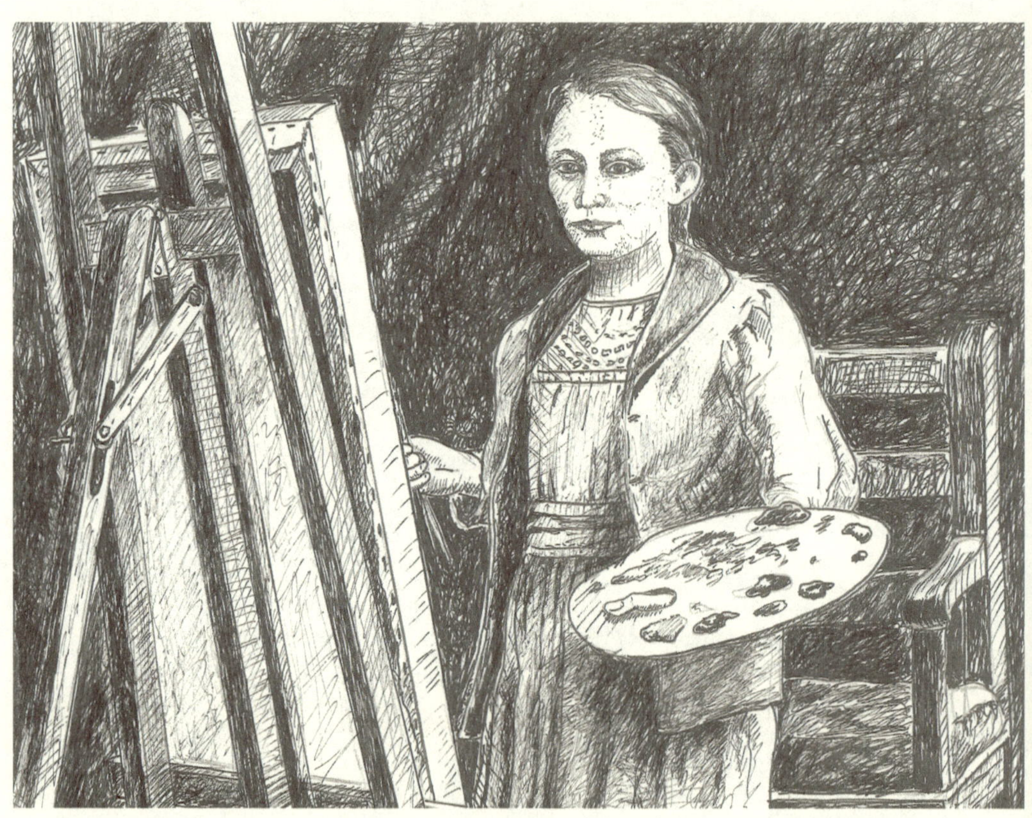

Georgia with a Palette

2

Nancy's Visits Near and in Abiquiu, New Mexico

My mother was preparing for my twelfth birthday celebration the summer of 1946 when I met fifty-nine year old Georgia in Abiquiu, New Mexico. My family does not remember the exact day, but we recalled that it was an event. Georgia walked through the garden gate at my Aunt Helen and Uncle Winfield's Rancho de Abiquiu to welcome us to the valley she had loved since 1931.

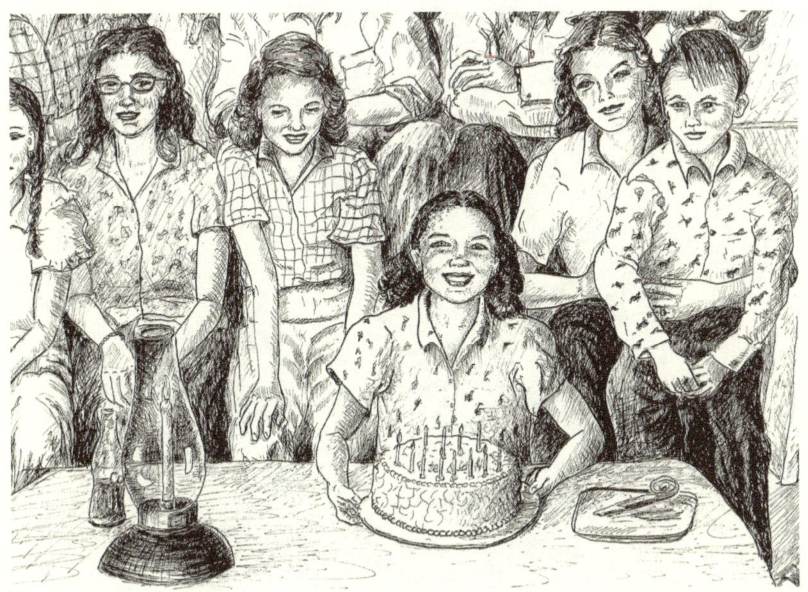

Nancy at Rancho de Abiquiu Celebrating Her Twelfth Birthday

By the time I was twelve years old in 1946, I knew the major role models of my life: my mother who gave birth to me, nurtured me, always made sure I was in the right place at the right time, and provided practicality with exuberance; and my Aunt Helen who welcomed me to participate in her events.

My recollection of our meeting Georgia included her black clothes worn for ease of movement and her face which had non-glamorous, strong angular surfaces. My youthful eyes took in everything I needed to know. She joined the ranks of my role models mother and aunt and left an "imprint" on me but in a faraway role.

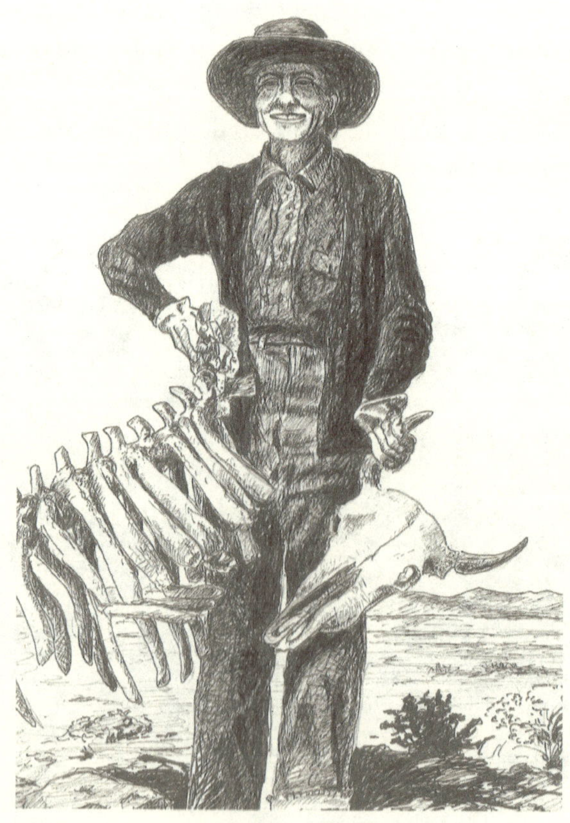

Georgia in Black

When I was nineteen years old in 1953, Aunt Helen, Uncle Winfield, Robert, Morten and I walked into the Abiquiu plaza on Christmas Eve. The plaza was aglow with the *luminarias* and *farolitos* as symbols to light the way for the coming Christ child.

I walked into Georgia's Abiquiu house that same Christmas Eve. With an innate ability to respond and act, I knew to look and see was my responsibility and only mine. Without saying a word to anyone, I thought to myself, "Something important is going on in this house."

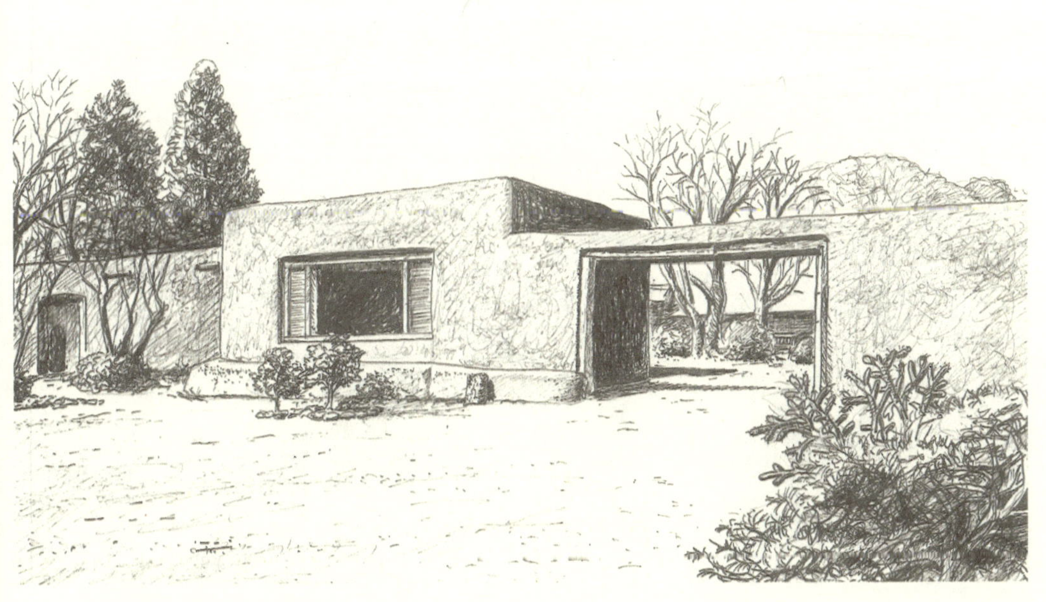

Georgia's Abiquiu House

As I was enjoying Christmas Eve, I noticed a painting on Georgia's white wall that was about three feet by four feet. On the rectangular white background was a blue ovoid shape that looked like a painting of a blue egg or an unfinished painting. From my perspective and young inner desire to draw some kind of conclusion, I tried to determine if the egg was representing an egg of a few thousandths of an inch or several inches. But I certainly knew it was a vivid blue. I was mesmerized by its beauty, elegance, simplicity, and artistry.

I left Georgia's house not knowing what I had seen. But I remembered and it did matter how I remembered, only that I didn't take my memory for granted. I was only human. Then, through the years I looked for the Blue Egg. It became important for me to find the painting. Was it a metaphor for something in my life, in my subconscious? Along the way I learned more and more about myself and Georgia.

3

Georgia's Career

Ida saw into the heart of Georgia, realized Georgia's natural talents, and instilled in her a love of learning. She assigned roles to each of her children according to their talents.

Georgia began early art lessons from Sarah Mann, a Sun Prairie neighbor and another strong, influential woman who employed the accepted method of copying well-known artists, to learn and improve Georgia's technique.

Georgia's early efforts were drawings in various media and small in nature. One teacher told her to not paint a hand so small. From then on, she painted large. It became important to help herself as much as she could because her work ethic related to her success.

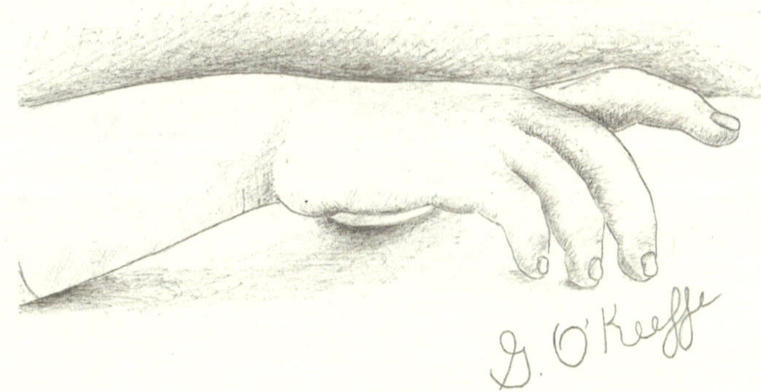

A Small Hand

Along the way in studying with different teachers, Georgia did not want to draw or paint what others had painted or drawn. Her artistic vision had no limitations.

Paint, brushes, oil, and watercolor became her words in an art world at the time dominated by men. She could reveal her feelings with color and shape, not with words, in both a representational and a pioneering abstract way with no guidelines and no labels.

The Rule of Thirds was only a beginning point as she worked a long time with an idea. The Rule of Thirds is a guideline requiring a format of square, rectangle, or oval divided into thirds horizontally and vertically. The center of interest is placed where these lines intersect. This creates motion, tension, interest, and energy.

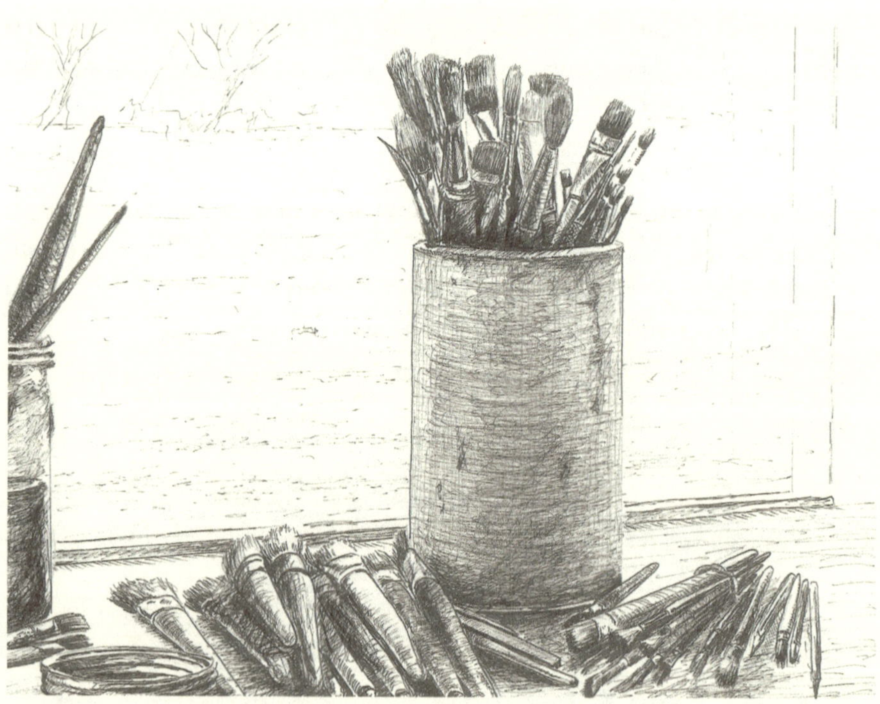

Paint Brushes

She repeated her subjects as a series: poppies, calla lilies, jimsonweeds, irises, New York skyscrapers, cow skulls, black crosses, doors in adobe walls, clouds, and even abstractions. She saw the earth as green and the sky as blue. Blue became her favorite color because it would always be there. Her totally nonverbal vision led her to believe everything she needed was in her surroundings.

By now Georgia, in setting her purposes and goals, used her inborn traits: imagination and unusual ideas, an easy use of her fingers to handle artist's tools, the ability to see everything around her and one thing at a time until she remembered it, the ability to see in two dimensions instead of three dimensions, and the ability to memorize all the shapes and colors. These traits would always be there when she called upon them.

Regardless of these talents, the time needed to be right, and coupled with a good portion of luck. Everyone has some type of talent, but the difference is the dedication to passionately follow through with the talent.

As Georgia advanced in her career, she taught art in Texas where she was introduced to light-drenched, multi-colored landscapes, vast spaces, and weathered bones. She spent much of her time painting in the outdoors. In addition to the landscapes, she painted straight bones, curved bones, discolored bones, bleached bones, and any hole in the bones allowed her to see through to what was beyond. She worked hard to be original and did not fear that being original made her different.

To Georgia, her vision appeared when she felt it even if others did not comprehend her vision. She distilled the complexity of her subjects into images of great simplicity. She painted very few individuals, preferring the desolate beauty of the desert, enlarged plants and flowers all infused with Surrealism, which she called "magical realism." The abstract art often did not represent objects or people from the observable world. She was later best known as a pioneer and was very influential in modernism.

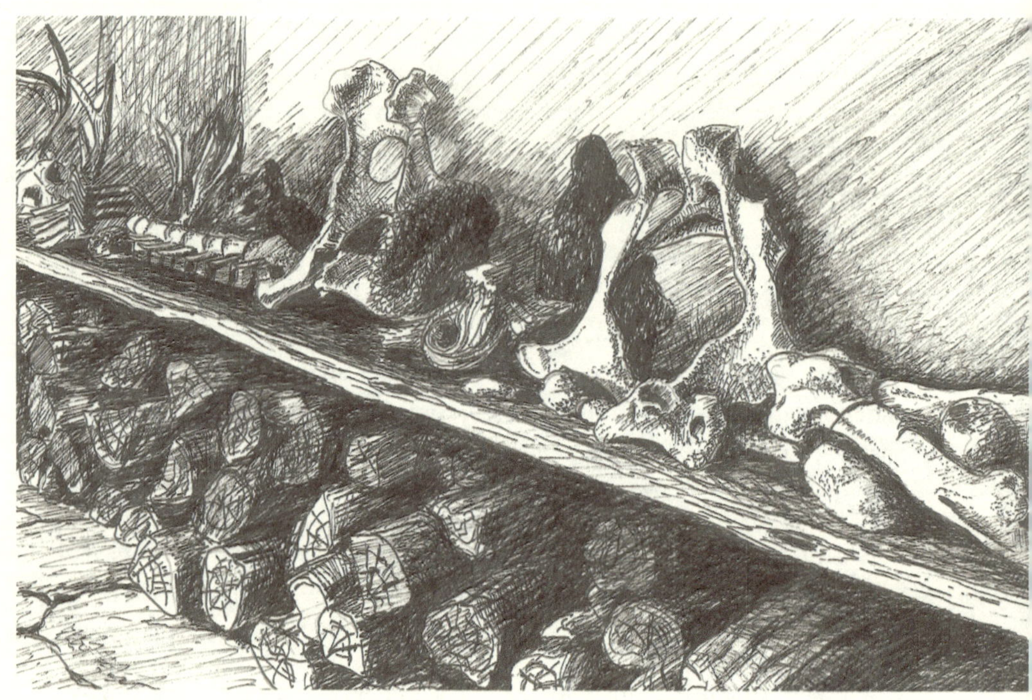

Bones

Later, when introduced to New Mexico she settled in Abiquiu where again she was surrounded by light, space, blue sky, and a landscape overpowered with multiple colors. Here she witnessed the vast process of invisible evaporation that gave the land its profile. In the dry sunlit landscape and clean air, she was attracted to more animal bones lying on the ground. She thought of them not as death, but live forms that had been rain-washed to white. She remarked, "The bones seem to cut to the center of something that is keenly alive on the desert even tho' the land is vast, and empty and untouchable and knows no kindness with all its beauty." She gave the bones a secret life.

Georgia focused on her sense of freedom as she painted in a variety of media such as oil, ink, and watercolor the magnified flowers as magical gems—rivers, trees, and mountains that changed the landscapes' character, bones, and abstractions. One part of a landscape by itself meant less than what it all looked together, all combined in her mind and eye's passion. Georgia wanted to be like a bird and when the limb broke, she would be okay because she had "wings."

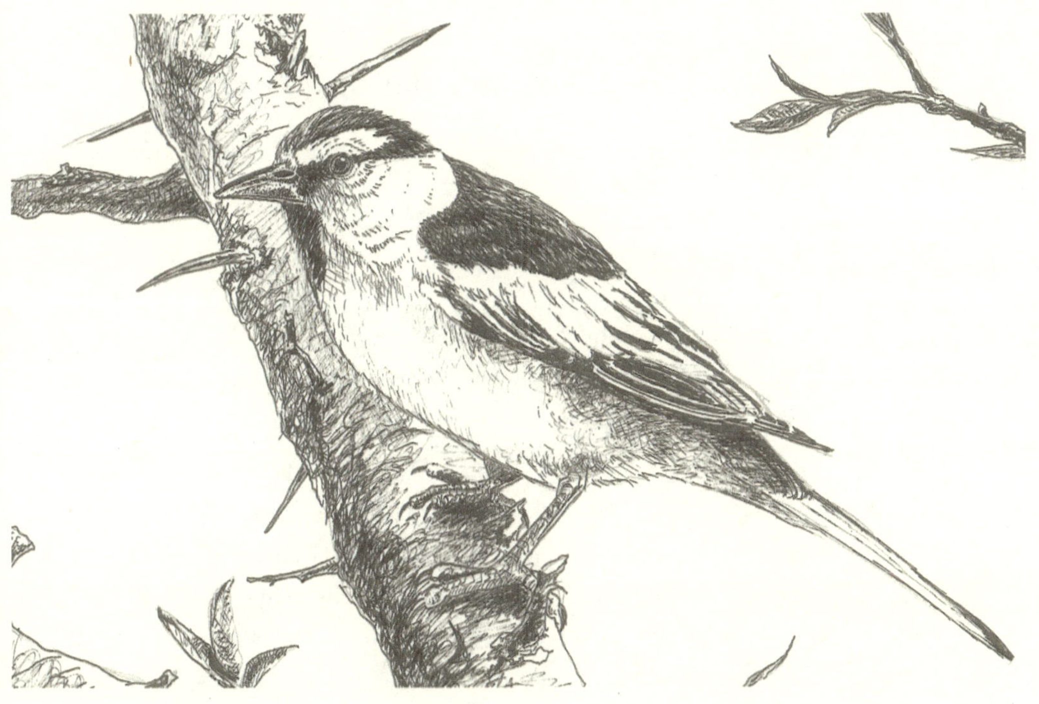

Bird on a Limb

4

Light Coming on the Plains and Nancy's Awakening Moment

With a 1955 marriage to Don Reily of Corrigan, Texas, I witnessed the change in my life with domesticity but no loss of my values and memories of the Blue Egg. There was no domination of one partner over the other. We were soul mates with the same moral values and the same relationship to nature and culture.

By 1966 Don and I had two children, nine year old Mark and seven year old Donna. I wanted the children to know of Georgia O'Keeffe. In 1966 the four of us drove the one hundred miles to Houston, Texas to see "Georgia O'Keeffe: An Exhibition of the Work of the Artist from 1915 to 1966" which had originally opened in Fort Worth, Texas. Aunt Helen and Uncle Winfield also attended the opening exhibition honoring Georgia. She inscribed one copy of the exhibition catalogue in a charming manner, "For Helen and her little Winfield with lots of love, Georgia."

My family walked through the Museum of Fine Arts, Houston and among others we saw three watercolors, *Light Coming on the Plains, No. I, No. II,* and *No. III,* all 11 x 8 inches, painted in 1917. Featured was *Pelvis Series, Red with Yellow,* 1945, oil on canvas, 36 x 48 inches. The bones as if a frame were held up to the sun and sky. But no Blue Egg in the exhibition. In my mind and imagination, the Blue Egg did not turn green or golden, but stayed true to Georgia's beloved color of blue.

Along the way I stayed focused, used my inborn traits of organization, enhanced my memory for design which is just paying attention, and kept my role models in sight.

I did not have a defining moment as Georgia did when she was twelve years old. My awakening moment in the search for the Blue Egg came when I was sixty-one years old, forty-nine years after I met Georgia. The Taos, New Mexico newspaper advertised on October 8, 1995 that the award winning journalist, Ralph Looney, would be signing autographs at the Brodsky Bookshop for his book, *O'Keeffe and Me, A Treasured Friendship.* I bought the book and Looney graciously inscribed the book. After I read of his close, delightful times with Georgia, I thought: I could write a book on Georgia because I had as many and more stories than Looney and maybe I would find my Blue Egg. I began what would become research on Georgia and my family's friendship.

After I arrived home I hurriedly retrieved from safekeeping Uncle Winfield's envelope marked, "Important - Georgia O'Keeffe." The envelope was full of Georgia's memorabilia, photographs, and letters. As true of most writing, I did not have to research my subject, only decide on how to select the form. I prepared my writing room library with two wooden book shelves full of books of various shapes and sizes creating a calm energy. I then assembled all the books I owned on Georgia and looked for the Blue Egg. I also gathered all related material and organized everything into my own personal retrieval system.

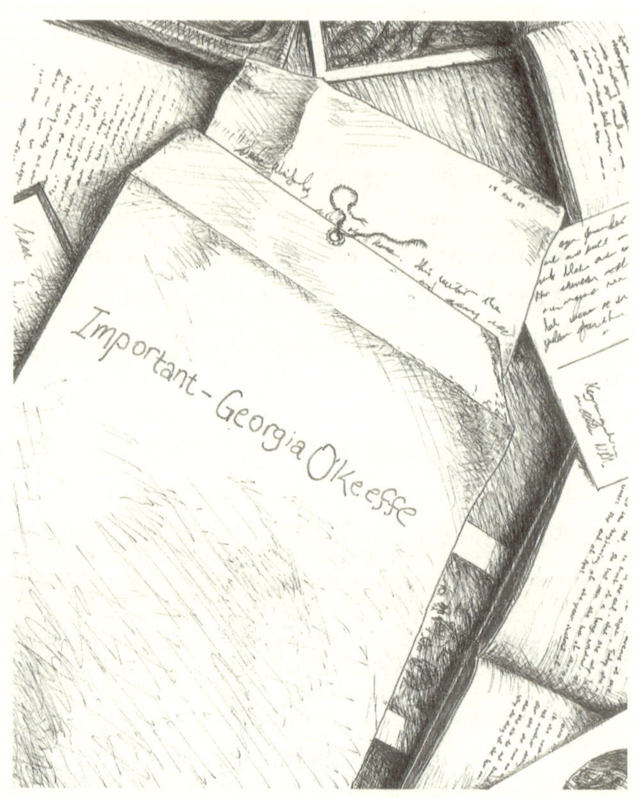

Winfield's Envelope

With this much accomplished I questioned: can it be done and can I do it? It could be done because I had available time, adequate resources, stamina, and the availability of archival material. I could do it, I assured myself, because I had the passion that resulted from knowing why I was writing—the same reason I read—to learn and discover the Blue Egg.

I began by putting what I knew into the computer's word processor, then diligently, systematically, patiently began researching. Research is not all that hard, as most people think—the trick is that you have to research a lot for accuracy and to add dimension to the story.

5

Georgia's Gift and Nancy's Research

Georgia had lived to be ninety-eight years old when she died in 1986. I rejoiced at meeting Georgia and I grieved when she died, but gave thanks for her life. The story of her birth and the length of her life was significant in what she accomplished. Her death, to me, was not the end of my story, but her death gave a changed meaning to all that came before.

Georgia possessed the ability to assemble all the elements in an uninhibited and independent manner with rhythm and balance into a blending known as "her style." She took from her role models whether they were traditional, non-traditional, or a combination of each a freedom of choice which was essential for her day-to-day growth. She created to fill her soul and when her soul was empty, she filled it again as she painted.

Georgia had said, "My painting is what I have to give back to the world for what the world gives me."

I had many spirited moments that fueled my passion. For me, the research trail was full of starts, stops, and detours. In my inexperienced days on the word processor I discovered at Yale University, New Haven, Connecticut that Fredrick W. Beinecke and his two brothers in 1963 had donated the Beinecke Rare Book and Manuscript Library. Imagine my amazement and delight at my word processing skills when I printed the entire fifty page collection catalogue for the Alfred Stieglitz/Georgia O'Keeffe Collection to discover three letters from Aunt Helen to Georgia.

When I visited the Yale University Beinecke Rare Book and Manuscript Library to research I was impressed at how the building of Vermont marble and granite was designed so the sun light was filtered to prevent the rare materials from being damaged. As I called for research papers from the research desk, I put on white cotton gloves to protect the material.

In July 1952 I attended the opening of the family-owned The Grand Imperial Hotel in Silverton, Colorado. For a century this building had been one of the finest examples of Victorian architecture. Built in 1882, it was nestled in a peaceful valley in southwestern Colorado known as the "Switzerland of America." The hotel had been renovated by my family for the 1952 opening. Many years later in our family's scrapbooks I discovered a menu for September 4, 1952 with Georgia's signature when she visited the hotel dining room. The friendship with my aunt and uncle was most evident.

I visited the Georgia O'Keeffe Museum in Santa Fe, New Mexico many times and on June 1, 2001 I met Jim Kuhlman at the gift shop. Kuhlman, from a pioneering Canyon, Texas family offered that from 1916 to 1918 his family owned unfenced land near Canyon where Georgia hiked on her way to Palo Duro Canyon. He gave me his insight into the land.

As I began writing my paper about the O'Keeffe research and the Blue Egg I had not had that one "defining moment" when I knew Georgia was seeking me. But it came in a flash on September 11, 2001.

The night before I had been inserting all my Beinecke Library research into the text. One of the items I photocopied was a letter dated August 10, 1933 from Dorothy Brett to Georgia after Georgia had an episode of psychoneurosis. In the letter Brett mentions that Georgia should read *The Way of All Women* by M. Esther Harding. As I inserted the material into the text several thoughts crossed my mind: was this book in Georgia's library, was the book still in print, and could I obtain a copy through the Interlibrary Loan system? The very next morning I picked up the October, 2001 issue of *New Mexico Magazine*. I skimmed through and I cannot explain why but I stopped on an article titled "Edith Wallace, Jung disciple still on quest for self-knowledge." Wallace was not a name I associated with Georgia. But tucked in the eighth paragraph I read, "It was also in London, in a second-hand bookstore on Tottenham Court Road, that Wallace picked up *The Way of All Women* by Esther Harding, a follower of Jung." I could not believe what I just read. I jumped up from the breakfast table and circled the halls in the house that was empty except for me. With no one to share my moment with, I declared with a racing heart: finding the mention of that book was my defining moment that I knew would come and I had been searching for to validate that Georgia was looking for me to tell our story.

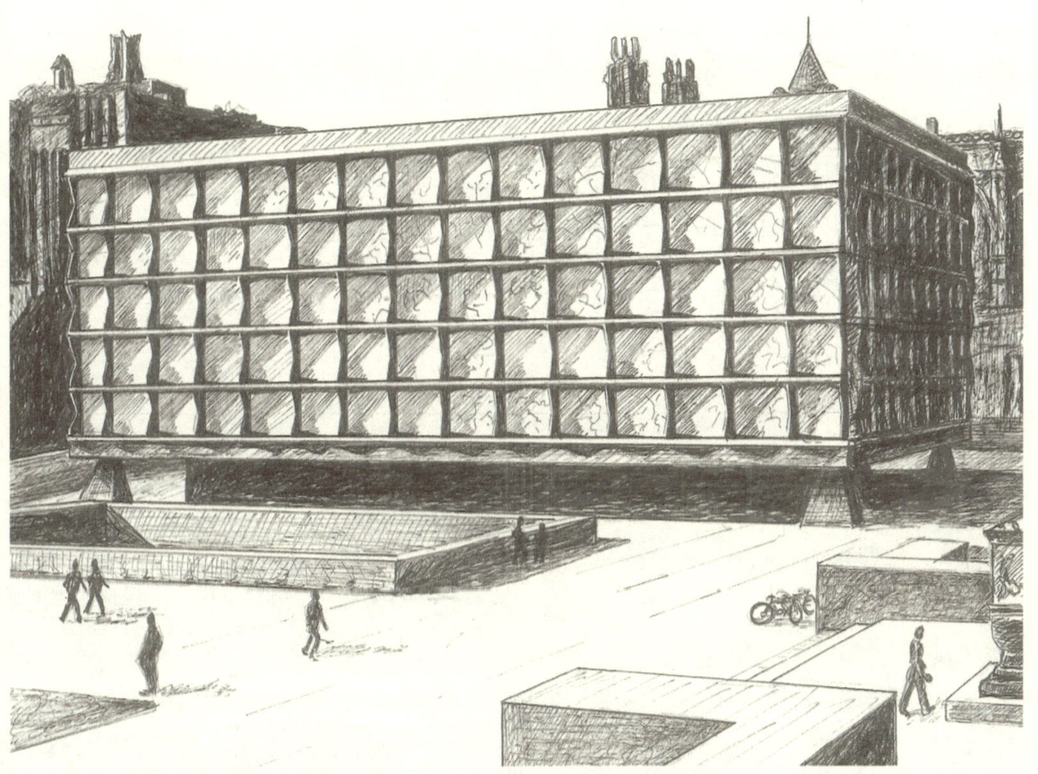

Yale University Beinecke Rare Book and Manuscript Library, New Haven, Connecticut

In New York City on January 17, 2002 Don and I wanted to go to the American Academy of Arts and Letters on Broadway between West 155th and West 156th Streets for research. It was north of Harlem and no taxi driver would take us through Harlem. Finally one taxi driver offered and when he left us, he gave us strict instructions where to stand for a safe taxi downtown.

The first literary and artistic elite organization in America eventually became known as the American Academy of Arts and Letters. Its aim was to advance art and literature. Georgia was awarded membership in 1966. After my research, the Academy personnel insisted they take us to our hotel in their private limousine.

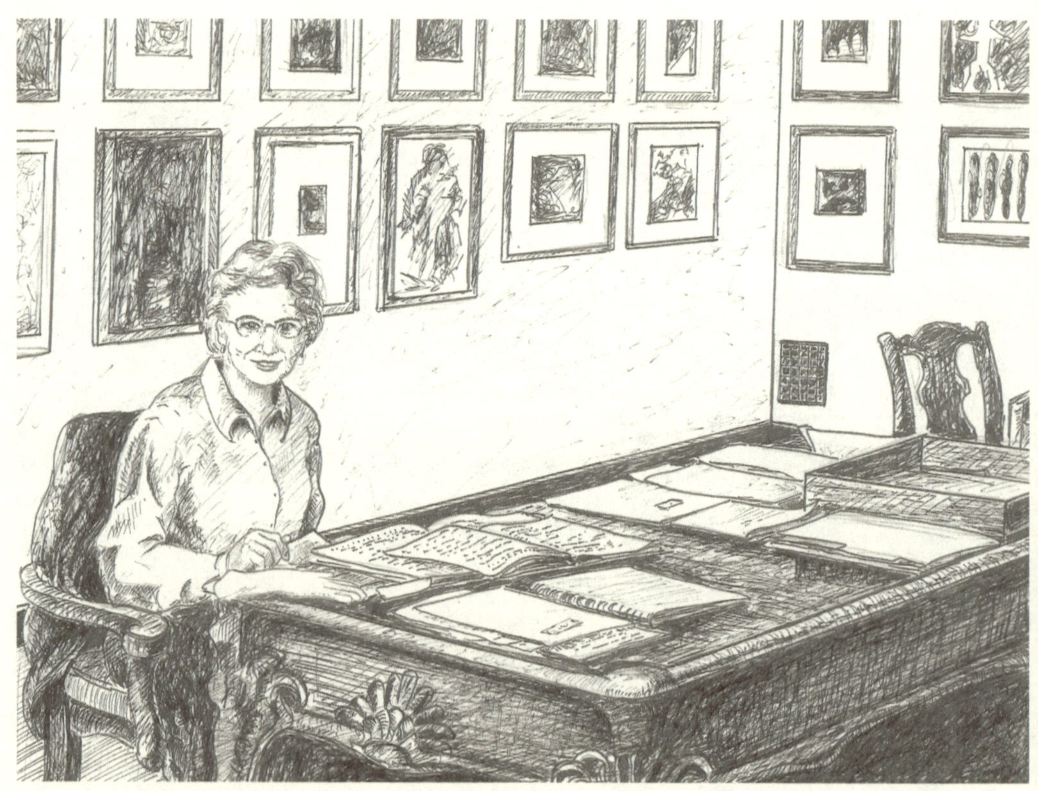

Nancy Researching at American Academy of Arts and Letters, New York City

Information seemed to be swirling around me. While visiting New York City during that same trip in January, 2002 Don, my friends Joan Duncan and Harry Stafford, and I had dinner reservations for 8:00 pm at Felida's at 243 East 58th Street. When we arrived we had to wait for about thirty minutes for our table. Standing next to our group of four were four New Yorkers who welcomed us and thanked us for coming to New York after September 11. They asked us, "Did we know ex-governor Ann Richards who lived above them?" Joan replied, "Yes, we were from the same high school in Waco, Texas." They asked us what we planned to do. I replied that I had some research on Georgia O'Keeffe at the American Academy of Arts and Letters. One woman remarked, "I worked on *Stieglitz and O'Keeffe*." I used my memory and I asked her, "Are you Benita Eisler?" She said, "No, I am Nan Talese and I also edited the Dorothy Norman book." The maitre'd called us to our table and I did not have an opportunity to talk to Nan. But I sat down at our reserved table amazed that of all the people in New York City I would stand next to a woman who edited books on Georgia. The timing was everything that evening and the circumstances were perfect. There was a sense of all the pieces coming together, but I did not yet know how. The Blue Egg was still a mystery.

On March 12, 2002 I was reading the endnotes for the research on Amarillo, Texas. I had emailed the Amarillo library reference department for a newspaper article. They could not find it. So I checked to be sure I had the correct date. Roxana Robinson's 1989 book *Georgia O'Keeffe, A Life*, page 578, endnote number 25 listed the books Georgia used at Canyon. One that was listed was the 1904 *How to Study Pictures* by Charles H. Caffin. The title sounded familiar.

Don's mother and father, Julia Belle and Gordon Reily, in the late 1940s bought a beautiful old home and acreage in Woodlake, Texas from a pioneering lumber family. It was furnished with the former owner's European furnishings of oriental rugs, crystal pieces, monogrammed linens, and books. When the Reilys sold the house in 1955 and built a house in Corrigan, Texas they brought many items from the Woodlake house. When the family moved out of the Corrigan house, the family selected items they wanted. Among the items I selected was a book *How to Study Pictures* by Charles H. Caffin. I was amazed that this book traveled quite a distance in time to reach me now that I needed it. Caffin wrote, "The world is full of beauty which many people hurry past or live in front of and do not see.... There is a world of beauty in pictures, but it escapes the notice of many, because, while they wish to see it, they do not know how.... The first necessity for the proper seeing of a picture is to try and see it through the eyes of the artist who painted it."

But the book did not give me any insight into finding the Blue Egg.

6

More Research for Nancy

All these experiences fueled my passion and forced me to further recognize that the story I was writing was seeking me. This is one facet of any research that has to be recognized, that there is a system of trails that leads and weaves every fact and experience together. The trail leads the seeker as if the answers are known to someone else.

There is a sense of direction that is indefinable and mysterious. Something beyond luck, timing, and even beyond hard work turns facts into extraordinary writing which allows the reader to perceive the world in a new way.

I felt the presence of Georgia in the room when I had lunch in the dining room of the Hudspeth House in Canyon, Texas. While Georgia was head of the art department at West Texas Normal College (now West Texas A&M University) from 1916 to 1918, she rented a room in Canyon. Georgia ate most of her meals at this boarding house. It was as if I wanted to capture the perfect atmosphere.

I had decided to visit Jerrie Newsom in Española, New Mexico in 1998. Jerrie was from Abiquiu and Aunt Helen trained her as a cook and housekeeper at Rancho de Abiquiu. Jerrie later worked for Georgia off and on for years in many capacities. Jerrie was among the last few people to see Georgia when she was in her last days in Santa Fe. When Jerrie greeted me in her mobile home she said, "Your presence is like your aunt's." She gave me familiar insight into the times and a few unpublished documents for safe keeping, but not a clue to the Blue Egg.

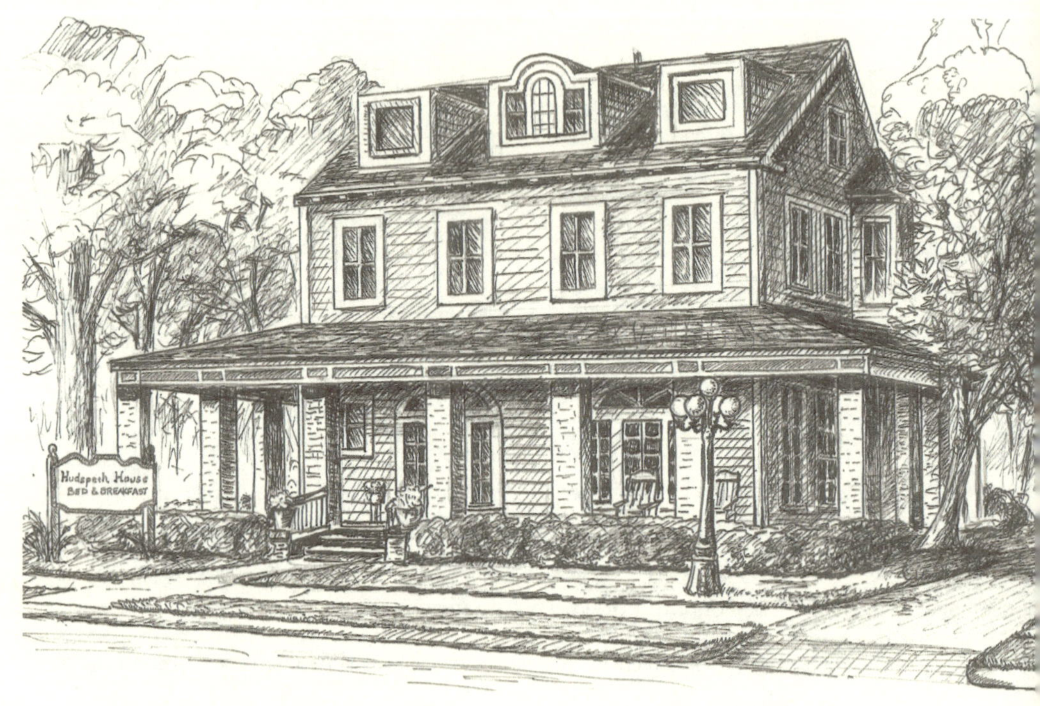

Hudspeth House, Canyon, Texas

In 2005 I called the Charlottesville, Virginia Historical Society for information and a map of the city during the time Georgia lived there on Wertland Street. Fred Dove answered the telephone. When I told him what I wanted he said, "I lived across the street from the house." We talked and he said he would take a picture for me if the Society did not have one. I waited to hear about a map from Margaret O'Bryant. When I did not hear from her I called the Society again. I was told that Fred Dove only worked on Tuesday afternoons. So I must have called him the first time on Tuesday afternoon. I called him the following Tuesday and he agreed to make photographs for me and send me extra material. How coincidental that I called the first time on a Tuesday, the only day Dove worked at the Society.

Meanwhile, earlier in 1964, I could not wait for perfect conditions, so

I drove on U.S. Highway 84 by Abiquiu to U.S. Forest Road 151 for fifteen miles on a road not navigable in rainy weather to the Benedictine Monastery of Christ in the Desert founded on the banks of the Chama River. Georgia had attended many of the services with the community of monks. After a quiet service, I spoke with the Abbott Phillip Lawrence for any clues to the Blue Egg, but he didn't have any information.

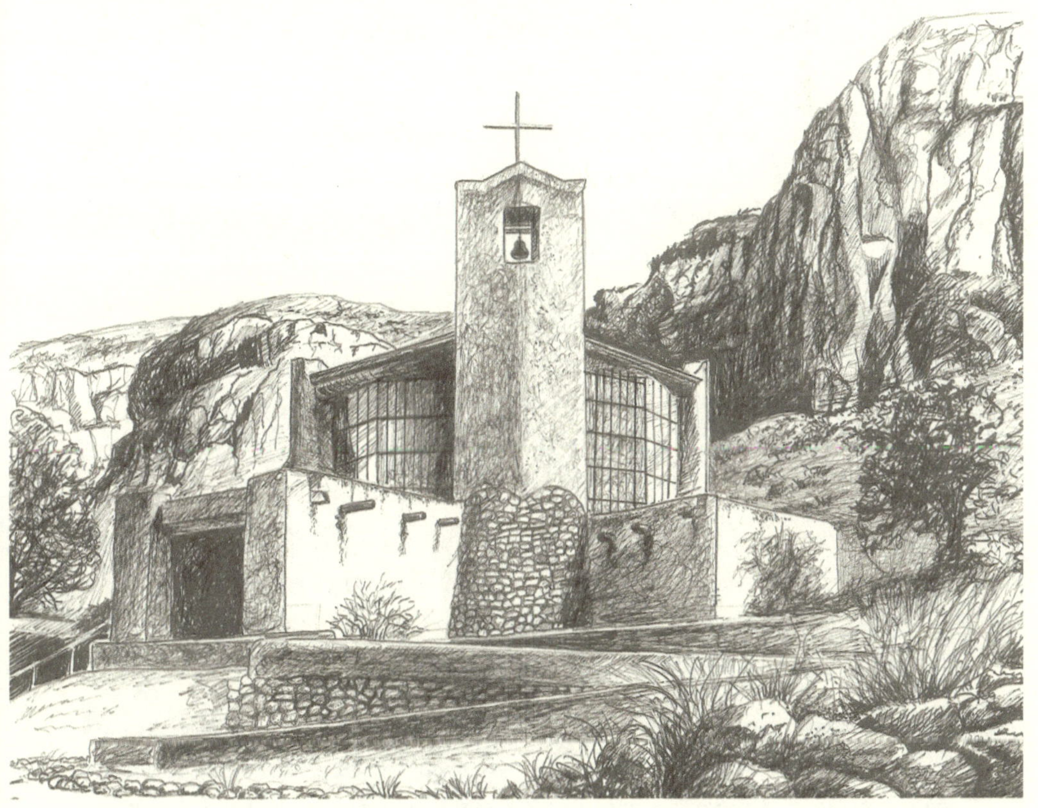

Monastery of Christ in the Desert near Abiquiu, New Mexico

I then wrote letters and received answers from Stanley Marcus of Neiman Marcus who had introduced my Aunt Helen to Winfield Morten in the 1930s. Carol S. Merrill, author of *O'Keeffe, Days in a Life* filled in many aspects of Georgia's life. When many unanswered letters filled my files, I thought maybe I was ahead of my time or had a bad sense of timing. Maybe the opportunities did not last forever but I was willing to risk making the time.

Over many months I walked the land and streets in Sun Prairie, Wisconsin, Amarillo and Canyon, Texas, and Abiquiu, Ghost Ranch and Taos, New Mexico. I visited Mabel Dodge Luhan's home in Taos where Georgia was introduced to other artists in New Mexico.

For thirty-seven years, not a short time, I witnessed research in the making at museums, art galleries, and in books but did not see the Blue Egg. I acquired certain flexibilities of my time and I did not waste my years by measuring my search or behavior on a scale of someone else's eyes. Yet I acquired these "researcher's tales."

As I searched, with each negative find of information came one positive clue to lead me forward. At times, the search made me forget about myself. Yet I could not deny the voice that called me to keep searching for the Blue Egg.

But by now I was researching for my book on Georgia and my family's friendship. "The how of my book" was as important as "the what of my book" as the research and book gathered steam. I was making an acquaintance with my book as I would with a person.

I wondered if I would ever find the Blue Egg. It was a specific task I set for myself, as if a forever planned event. I was transferred from my comfortable, warm days to worlds beyond my experience. As I traveled to the Four Corners Region and the Bisti/De-Na-Zin Wilderness area in northwest New Mexico, it was as if once I started climbing a steep, rough terrain the only option was to keep my mind on the boulders and finish the climb. But my goal was the Blue Egg. Georgia often traveled to the Bisti to paint in the desolate area of steeply eroded badlands which she called "The Black Place."

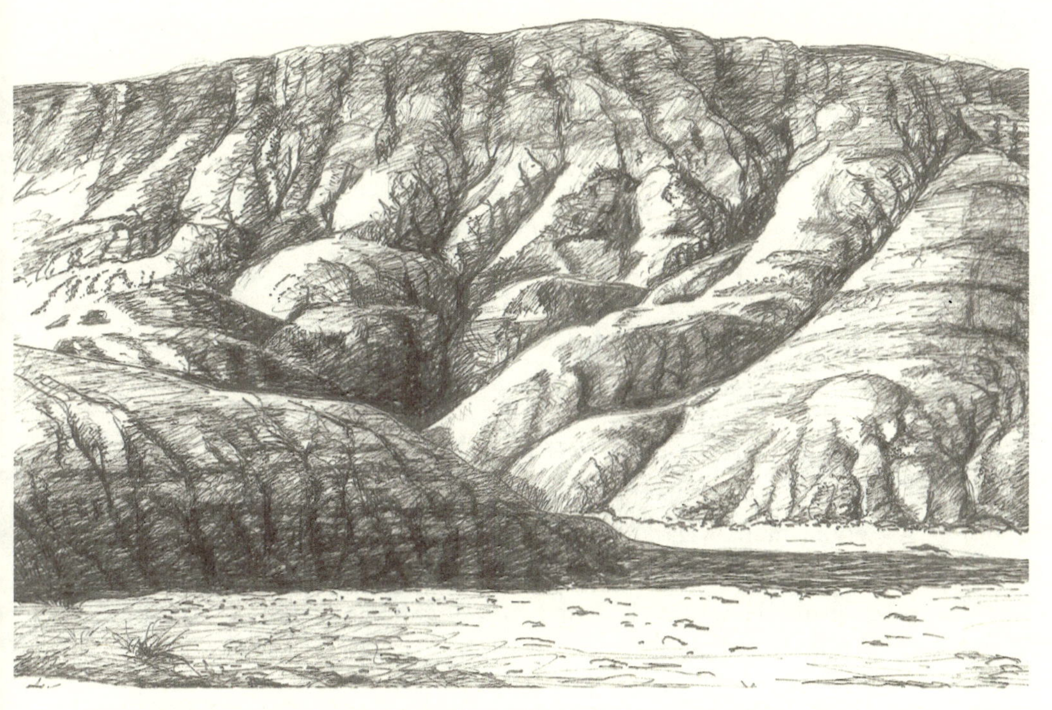

The Bisti/De-Na-Zin Wilderness, "The Black Place" in New Mexico

The journey of searching was a joy that I savored. I wanted to finish the search for the Blue Egg which had prompted my writing the two volume book on Georgia.

The thrill of seeing my published books occupy the shelves of the Georgia O'Keeffe Museum gift shop was overwhelming. I even offered to autograph them and told the gift shop people my Texas friends were always asking where to buy my books–at the gift shop. Then came the request from the New Mexico Museum of Art, Fray Angélico Chávez History Library to donate my O'Keeffe research to their library. With Don and my grandson, Thomas Reily, we sorted files and boxed sixteen boxes of research to ship to the library.

7

The Blue Egg in a Book

Years later, I opened the 1985 book *The Art & Life of Georgia O'Keeffe* by Jan Garden Castro. There on page 151 was a black and white photograph by Jack Holmes of Georgia in the fall of 1950 sitting at a desk at Alfred Stieglitz's New York City's An American Place. To my surprise, in the background, hanging on a white wall, was the painting of my Blue Egg.

When I saw it, I realized that here, finally, was what I had been searching for–the Blue Egg I had seen in 1953 hanging on the white wall as a newly painted work of art in Georgia's Abiquiu home.

Through the years she had painted pelvis bones from different angles, using her adored color blue. The skulls had been painted as if floating on the canvas and so real I wanted to reach out to grab them. As always, her vision and interpretation of the subject she loved was pared to the essentials and the fragment was better than the whole. The blue ovoid shape that I thought was a blue egg all these years ago, was the blue sky as seen through the sun bleached white pelvis bone opening. I realized that Georgia liked to see into and through the bones. Without a marshmallow cloud formation in the blue sky, it was as if Georgia exclaimed about her piece of the blue sky, "I am the sky."

In Georgia's early days in Texas and New Mexico she had seen new things and been attracted to and collected the bones of animals lying on the Texas plains and New Mexico desert. After more than a trilogy series of paintings featuring bones, not death, but shapes and forms, her next to last bone painting was *Pelvis Series,* oil on canvas, 40 x 48 inches, 1947. Today the Blue Egg is on the white, polished page 722 of the 1999 Barbara Buhler Lynes' *Georgia O'Keeffe: A Catalogue Raisonné, Volume II.*

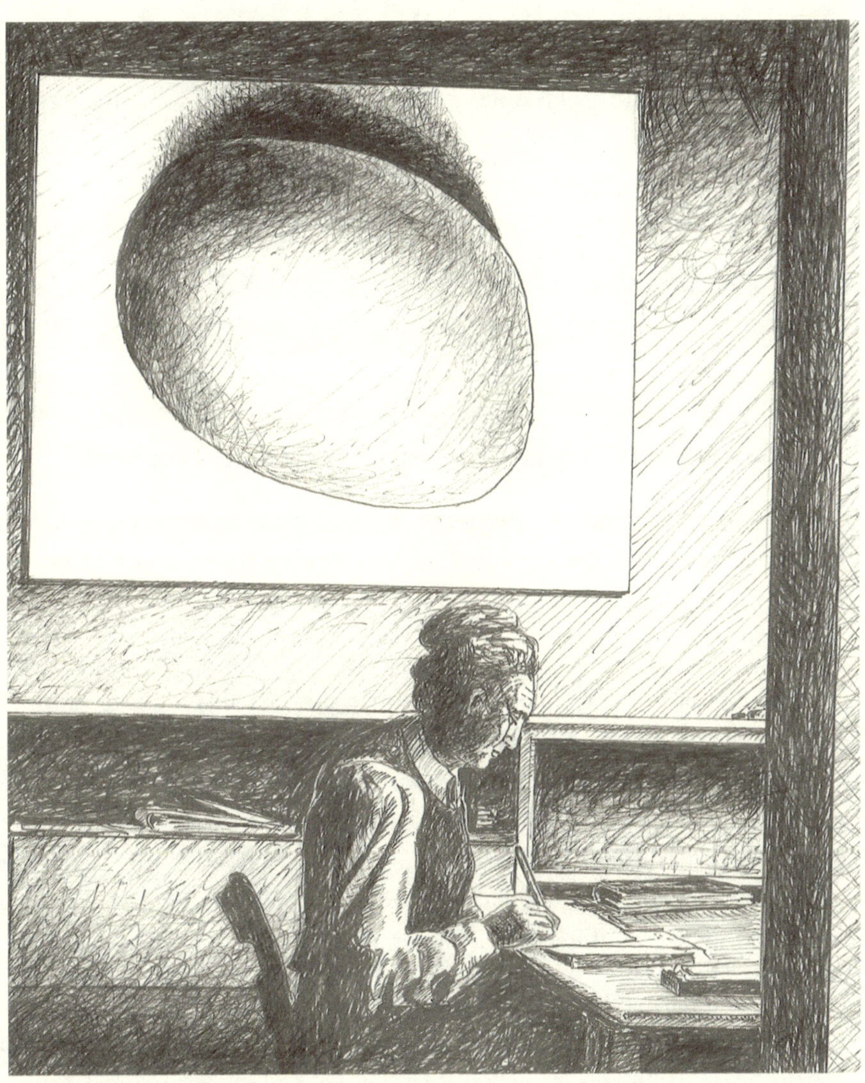

The Blue Egg in a Book

I was not prepared for the utter delight in the discovery for which I had longed. Upon finding the Blue Egg my brain lit up as if I had painted the Blue Egg myself.

An egg is an egg.

An egg is an egg until it becomes a blue egg representing something else.

An egg is an egg until I see its ovoid shape as self-expression.

That egg that becomes blue, ovoid, and self-expression teaches me.

Enlightenment through the beauty of a framed blue sky.

Why did I search for so many years for the Blue Egg I saw in 1953? Maybe, now that I have identified the painting, my insight must follow.

Today, the journey of discovery, with no road map or GPS, makes sense. I realize that everything I had early in my life is still intact–curiosity, role models, memories, and an inborn trait to be a good listener, yet wanting to be heard.

In spite of time I remain curious, unafraid of change in perception of the Blue Egg actual painting and my initial impression of what it represented. My initial curiosity became the lifeblood of my journey and I did not turn my back. Time did not hush my curiosity or take away my curiosity but my intellectual curiosity grew fast and furious. My natural young desire for knowledge evolved and after the discovery, turned into satisfaction. If I had not been curious, I would not have known that the long journey made sense.

Role models come in all different forms. There are people who leave an imprint on you. Family role models accept their responsible role and influence as a social role of arriving at the right place, to which I aspire. With self-confidence and exposure I formed through the years a role model mindset of Georgia because I noted how she did something well. It became easy to think of another's life which led me to think of my own life. The journey of finding the painting, and along the way, finding more of myself, was exciting as it became a question of identity and relationships.

The search to find the Blue Egg enhanced my capacity to be a good listener and to never spend days crying, but to be heard. Everyone wants to be heard from the beginning. When I am heard, all else seems quiet.

As I revisited my youth, I did not want to lose the memories of my happy childhood as it unfolded and defined me. My childhood inner realizations of the beauty of my surroundings assured me that memories are not taken for granted. It does matter how I remember things as I integrate the present with the past. The past is a part of me and belongs to me. The past of searching for the Blue Egg and its subsequent writings is never over and all its avenues are not over because they sparkle in my heart.

To surrender to the wonder of this story and of all the interesting people I met and all the places I traveled and to finish this truly, true story of my journey is to be joyful which is a powerful force. How could this journey of discovery not persuade the reader to learn from these lives and not stimulate and enlighten the reader for their own discovery?

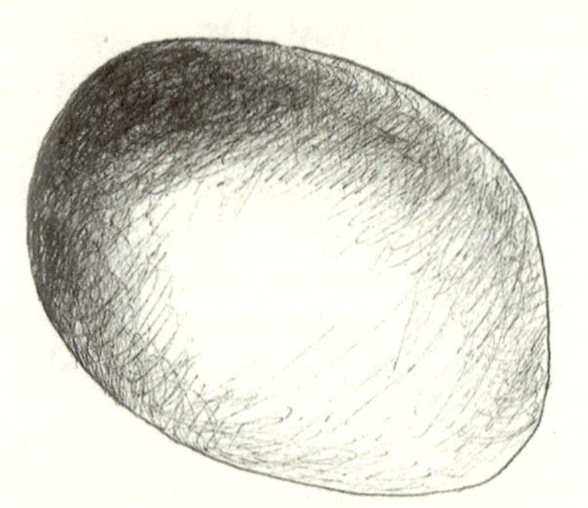

About the Author

Nancy Carolyn Hopkins Reily writes of viewing a painting at Georgia O'Keeffe's Abiquiu, New Mexico home on Christmas Eve, 1953. As a nineteen year old woman, Reily wondered what the painting was—an unfinished painting or a blue egg. But she realized that something important was going on in the house.

One viewing of anything can spark steps for a journey lasting a day, weeks or years. Reily takes you on her long, long journey of discovery of the painting she called "The Blue Egg." The journey took her to the Georgia O'Keeffe Museum where she met a landowner where Georgia had walked its awe inspiring landscape in Canyon, Texas; the Yale University Beinecke Rare Book and Manuscript Library in New Haven, Connecticut; an interview with Georgia's retired cook, Jerrie Newsom, in Jerrie's mobile home; a visit to the Monastery of Christ in the Desert; introducing her two children to search at the Museum of Fine Arts, Houston; research that ended in the Georgia O'Keeffe Museum gift shop with on the shelves her two books on Georgia; being asked to donate her research to the New Mexico Museum of Art, Fray Angélico Chávez History Library; and the final steps of packing sixteen boxes of research to be shipped to the Fray Angélico Chávez History Library.

While Nancy was in elementary school, her mother introduced her to books when she took her to the Lakewood Branch of the Dallas Public Library. This viewing unbeknownst to Nancy began a long, long journey about books and words.

After a 1955 B.B.A. degree from Southern Methodist University, then marriage, homemaking, and children, Nancy embarked on a quest to find that indescribable force within herself to say something that couldn't be said verbally. She began a career as an outdoor color photography portraitist where she learned to not just look, but to see.

Nancy began her interest in writing when she recorded the Robert Louis Stevenson's quote, "A friend is a gift from you to yourself." She added hundreds of other sayings and in a rare moment of what to do with her notes, she literally "cut and pasted" the sentences together and decided to write a book using the thoughts. She had turned her ability to see into writing which is just another way to see. In 1990 she published all these thoughts based on her experiences in the New Mexico and Colorado mountains.

Through the years, Nancy's interest in words has led to researching sixty-four lines of family genealogy before Ancestry.com, keeping a daily journal since 1976, and simply organizing research into books on many subjects.

If asked, "How long did it take to write *The Blüe Egg*," she replies, "My age at the time."

Nancy Hopkins Reily was born in Dallas, Texas about mid-way between the Great Depression of 1929 and 1941 when the United States entered World War II. She was named after a *McCall's* magazine story with the heroine named Nancy, a name her mother liked. With two brothers she didn't play dolls, but played baseball and football in the neighborhood, caught fireflies at night, and climbed the low branch tree in their yard. Since childhood, Reily has divided her time between Texas, Colorado and New Mexico. Her college education began at Gulf Park College, Gulfport, Mississippi and ended with a B.B.A. degree from Southern Methodist University. After college she joined the ranks of marriage, homemaker and motherhood. This led to a career of volunteering for many organizations. She is the author of *Classic Outdoor Color Portraits, A Guide for Photographers*; *Georgia O'Keeffe, A Private Friendship, Part I, Walking the Sun Prairie Land*; *Georgia O'Keeffe, A Private Friendship, Part II, Walking the Abiquiu and Ghost*

Ranch Land; *Joseph Imhof, Artist of the Pueblos* with Lucille Enix, *My Wisdom That No One Wants*, and *Half-Past Winter*, all from Sunstone Press, and *I Am At An Age* with Lucille Enix, Best of East Texas Publishers. Reily makes her home in Lufkin, Texas.

About the Artist

Byron Jones has specialized in professional mural painting and is recognized in Texas as one of the leading artists in his field. Though his subject matter varies, he has a passion for western and wildlife subjects. Having spent much of his time in the outdoors while growing up in Texas, Byron has a particular affinity for these two areas.

This book has been printed on acid free paper.

The typeface is Goudy OldStyle.

Goudy OldStyle is a classic typeface originally created by Frederic W. Goudy for American Type Founders (ATF) in 1915. It is a graceful, balanced design with a few eccentricities, including the upward-curved ear on the g and the diamond shape of the dots of the i, j, and the points found in the period, colon and exclamation point, and the sharply canted hyphen. Certain of its attributes—most notably the gently curved, rounded serifs of certain glyphs—suggest a Venetian influence.

www.ingramcontent.com/pod-product-compliance
Lightning Source LLC
LaVergne TN
LVHW051021080826
845145LV00009B/2742

* 9 7 8 1 6 3 2 9 3 2 0 2 0 *